Airedale Terrier

By
Holland Buckley

Vintage Dog Books
Home Farm
44 Evesham Road
Cookhill, Alcester
Warwickshire
B49 5LJ

www.vintagedogbooks.com

ISBN No. 978-1-84664-036-0

Published by Vintage Dog Books 2006
Vintage Dog books is an imprint of Read Books

British Library Cataloguing-in-Publication Data
A catalogue record for this book is available
from the British Library.

Vintage Dog Books
Home Farm
44 Evesham Road
Cookhill, Alcester
Warwickshire
B49 5LJ

THE
AIREDALE TERRIER

By

HOLLAND BUCKLEY

(FOURTH EDITION)

MANCHESTER:

"OUR DOGS" PUBLISHING COMPANY, LIMITED,

4, Albert Square.

———

1913.

G. H. ELDER.

Dedicated to

GEORGE H. ELDER

(Vice-President of the S.O.E.A.T. Club).

Now, and for Many Years, one of the Bulwarks

of the Breed, a *persona grata* in all

ranks of the Fancy, and a

Steadfast and Strenuous Friend

to the Author.

HOLLAND BUCKLEY.

Preface.

Iᴛ is barely forty years ago since this, the largest breed of the Terrier family, was evolved, by the efforts of a few enthusiasts in Yorkshire, from a Witches' Cauldron mixture of Otterhound, the Welsh Harrier, and, in all probability, the Bull-terrier, the chief object being to breed a dog that could live in the water and tackle any-thing from a rat to an otter with unflinching gameness It is possible that the Sheepdog played some part in the manufacture. Breeders of recent years have ofttimes wished that the founders of the breed had been rather less catholic in their materials. All credit must be given to them for producing in so short a time a dog good to look at, and at the same time a good workman. Present-day admirers are lucky in their generation, nearly all litters now being fairly uniform in type and general all-round excellence. It was not so many years ago, one could, had he so minded, have benched specimens from any one litter in Airedale classes, Old English Terriers (alas! now de-funct), Otterhounds, and Welsh Terriers, with a fair prospect of winning honours. Even now tragic reminders of the bar sinister will appear in the shape of dun-coloured pups in the most classic litters. The stumbling-block in the path of this fascinating breed has been for years the coat, but now, after long years of weary endeavour, a real natural wire jacket, straight in lay, is the reward of those-breeders who have scientifically bred sheep coats out of their favourites. Fanciers who have never deviated from the cult of sound coats or nothing can now look upon the present agitation against trimming with perfect and happy indifference. An Airedale, bred on correct modern lines, needs no tonsorial aid, and is, without doubt, the happier for it. And after all that is the first consideration of a real fancier, whether his favourite be a pet or a workman. The idea that clever trimming will deceive an experienced judge is really laughable. Try it on with any of our front rank judges, and you will be fired out of the ring, with an unsympathetic reference to the show being a month too soon for your shorn Terrier. A broken coat can, no doubt, to the casual eye, cover a multitude of sins, and sometimes a sausage body; but how any expert can cover up, by trimming, defects of make and shape is one of those things, as Lord Dundreary would say, " no fellah can understand "—always allowing, of course, that the judge is a capable one. An adjudicator who knows his business will always penalise exhibits trimmed up for his deception. There are certain lines of blood that make for sheep coats. Breeders have themselves wholly to blame if they breed to those lines. A smooth coated bitch of modern breeding is the best asset a fancier can have in his kennel.

Quite a lot of nonsense has been written of late years upon the size, chiefly by individuals who never owned a good Terrier, and have not the nous to breed one; and in the highly improbable event of having raised something out of the common, would more than likely (such is the windbag's crass ignorance!) sell their best for a waster. In this connection I vividly remember one of these ignoramuses who, having used a well-known champion stud dog, brought the pride of the litter for my admiration. I knew my man, and therefore ventured diffidently to suggest that the pup's skull would go coarse. The reply given, with intense earnestness, was, " Leave that to me; I'll stop it." The very easiest point of all to obtain is size, and the hardest point, quality. I have never yet known a lasting front ranker who was a big one. I read a very able letter in *Our Dogs* on this point from a well-known breeder, who very fairly reasoned, with sound logic, that size was purely relative.

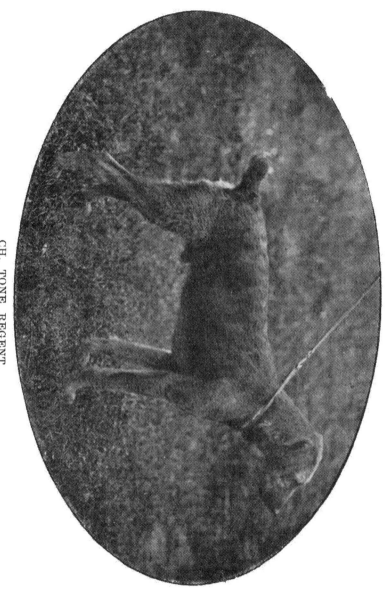

CH. TONE REGENT.

Clonmel Monarch was considered by the cognoscenti—
" good old cognoscenti "—small ; yet, when he matured,
which was not until he was two years, he tipped the beam
at forty-five pounds. At twelve months he was barely
thirty-seven pounds. And yet, at that age, he downed a
great many champions, of all breeds, in variety competition. Much the same applies to another great Terrier
in his day, Ch. Arthington Tinner, and yet fit
to-day he scales forty-six and is a laster. The truth of
it is, that some lines of blood produce Terriers who
mature late. A fine instance of this is the great stud dog,
Ch. Master Briar. Had he been made up in his youth,
like the leggy, flat-sided brigade, who are admired simply
for their size, he would probably never have known
defeat, but he would not in that case have lasted like he
has to-day. Willow Nut, Colne Crack, Venus, and, of
latter days, Clonmel Bedrock, Tone Masterpiece, Legrams
Prince, Otley Chevin, and Tone Jerry, would not in their
young days have drawn the weight they should have
done, according to the quidnuncs of the fancy, but they
all made up to the standard when matured. Many
instances could be given of well-known dogs who were
absolute standard weight at twelve months, but too big
for the bench afterwards. Two notable instances that
come to mind easily are Briar Wood and Clonmel Gamecock ; perhaps in Briar Wood's case fortunately for
breeders, his time being profitably employed in getting
champions. The chief reason that tends to make the
Airedale the most popular Terrier of the day is, no doubt,
that the devoted band who have stuck to him through
thick and thin, and improved him into the strikingly
handsome dog that he is to-day, have never forgotten
that he is, *par excellence*, a sporting Terrier, and have
paid even more attention to this side of his many-sided
character, and that is largely the reason of his vast
popularity, especially in country sporting districts. The

breed is well supplied with clubs, and the latest educational movement of the South of England A.T.C., in establishing the London and District branch, is a huge success. Match nights are always largely attended. The novice and the beginner has many object lessons brought before him at these gatherings, so that they are of incalculable benefit. They have been time and again exclusively catered for by shows being organised on strict novice lines. The value of this sort of show cannot be overestimated, and, in this respect, the lines of latter-day fanciers are indeed cast in pleasant places. Vigilant care should be bestowed on coat and contour, combined with size and quality. I must strenuously impress upon breeders to stick to the black back and golden tan, which in combination is so charming, and also quite characteristic of the breed. In conclusion, I have a profound conviction that the Airedale has come to stay.

HOLLAND BUCKLEY.

CH. LEGRAMS PRINCESS.

CH. CLONMEL MONARCH.

Index to Chapters.

Index to Illustrations.

E. ROYSTON MILLS.

President South of England Airedale Terrier Club

THE AIREDALE TERRIER.

CHAPTER I.

Origin and History.

The absolute origin of the breed is "wrapped in a good deal of mystery." The conviction is shared by a great many fanciers that the Welsh Harrier played a leading rôle in the first instance in the production of our favourite, and without a shadow of doubt to the Welsh Harrier's first cousin, the Otterhound, we are largely, if not solely, indebted for the Airedale's many excellences as a water dog. To me it is calamitous that we should be in danger of losing that thick, piley undercoat, which is oily in its nature. A coat of this sort will stand any amount of water, and then only appear half wet. The manufacturers of the breed were evidently in dead earnest on this point, for in the original standard great stress was laid upon the weather-resisting qualities of the ideal jacket, and the majority of points were awarded for the coat taken as a whole. Old-time fanciers were also not near so keen on that cat-foot which we now insist upon, arguing, and very justly so, that since the work was chiefly in the water, a foot tending more to the web-shape was one of the chief desiderata in swimming. It was undoubtedly these sporting qualities in the water that enabled the breed to make its way at the rapid rate we have seen, and that without the booming of the fancier press that so largely helped other varieties. Thirty-five years ago the Airedale was a *rara avis* outside the broad County of Yorkshire, and he was mostly known by the name of the Working Terrier or Waterside Terrier. It was no uncommon sight to see quite 200 entries at shows like Bingley. At one of these shows a meeting was called and the breed given the euphonic title of the Aire dale Terrier. There was about this time a good deal of correspondence in the "Live Stock Journal." All this excited a great amount of interest, and the breed enlisted some powerful supporters in its best interests. A vast deal of harm was inflicted upon the breed at this time by the descriptive article which appeared in the "Book of the Dog." Mr. Reginald Knight was the author of the article, giving a description and scale of points which, as Mr. C. H. Mason caustically wrote, probably fitted his dog Thunder, but was radically wrong in many respects.

It was Mr. Mason who probably had the honour of taking the first specimen to the United States in Bruce, who was the father of Champion Brush, a very useful animal at stud, although blind in one eye, but one of the gamest Terriers that ever lived. It will come as a surprise to latter-day fanciers that the gameness of the breed was hotly debated. Breeds that are quarrelsome often get a spurious reputation for great pluck, so that the mild aloofness of the Airedale was by some set down to lack of spirit, but his grim readiness to take death with unflinching courage soon placed him in the forefront as a courageous companion who would not quarrel unless "put upon." There are few breeds where the element of personal devotion is so pronounced, and any lonely country house guarded by one or two Airedales would be given a wide berth by the burgling fraternity. His greatest claim as a sporting dog is his all-round character as a field dog. And here, considered historically, he has not deteriorated one iota from his adaptability to every line of sport as a gun-dog. He is seldom or never gun shy, and will do, if properly trained, the work of the Pointer, Setter, Spaniel, and Retriever. As a rabbit dog he is *facile princeps*. So here we have lost none of his original sporting qualities. One often

CH. TONE MASTERPIECE.

hears the old-time idols in the different breeds spoken of as being so much the superior of latter-day specimens. However true this may be of other breeds, it most surely does not hold good of the Airedale great prize winners like Rustic Twig, Young Tanner, Tanner, Rover, Newbold Fritz, Rustic Lad, Venom, Vixen III., and Rustic Kitty. Vixen no doubt was nearer to our ideals than the rest, but she would not have compared, in my opinion, with the best of later days. Ch. Dumbarton Lass, Ch. Broadlands Bashful, Ch. Dumbarton Sceptre, Ch. Mistress Royal, or Clonmel Coronation would, without a question, have been very far in advance, and as great a dog as Ch. Cholmondeley Briar was in his prime, considered as a Terrier, Ch. Clonmel Monarch would have been an easy winner. Cholmondeley Briar was certainly one of the soundest dogs within my memory. This is the Terrier who put up the record of winning a cup eleven times, and to the real grief of the writer, just failing to win it for the twelfth and final occasion. Ch. Clonmel Marvel was the victor, thus proving the old adage that youth will be served. I am happy to relate that by the kindness of the Committee of the Airedale Terrier Club a way was found, and the cup found its final resting-place on the sideboard of Briar's owner, who was himself a tower of strength to the breed when it was in vital need of it.

Mr. H. M. Bryans, perhaps more than any other leading fancier, established a type and an insistence upon make and shape combined with real Terrier quality, and I have a letter before me now in which he very generously gives full credit to the fanciers of to-day in their efforts on the same lines. Unquestionably the most pleasing task that can fall to the lot of the striver after perfection is to chronicle the steady and persistent improvement of type and quality of one's favourites. I yield to none in my admiration for the old lights of the ring; but, truth to tell, we have advanced, and for the one or two great Terriers in the years that are past who used to fight their duels at show after show the fancy can now pit together a score of front rankers, all so close together that the lucky first of one day is the reserve of the next. I don't know that it is in my province, yet I must strenuously warn breeders that in their keen desire to get that high quality and Terrier character, they are sacrificing that beautiful black saddle, with its pig bristle harshness. A dog with a coat like this can be hours in the water without materially altering the feel, and I am keen that it never should be forgotten that the Airedale is, *par excellence*, a water dog. But to enable him to keep that just title we must breed for the weather-resisting jacket. Yorkshire fanciers have not abated one jot in their interest for the breed. One of the sights of the year for the pessimistic owner is the great Airedale carnival at Otley, in June, to see the vast ring crowded on the outside, six deep, with men and women, following with breathless interest the various results, many of the spectators probably knowing just as much about the breed as the adjudicator. Time was, and not so very far back, when party feeling ran so high that the judge who displeased the home experts around the ring side was often in imminent danger of personal ill-usage. I remember on one very sultry occasion when a popular judge, and a very much respected one of the day, had to beat a hasty retreat. That rare old dog, Clip, was the cause of the popular clamour of that day. For my own part, I always thought the judge unjustly assailed, as, even according to present-day requirements, Clip would be considered a first flighter. One great good this old warrior did for the breed in general, and a to-day celebrated kennel, was to stamp his beautiful dark eyes upon the breed, and that at a time when the Hound-like shape and colour were very prevalent. Poor old Clip

CROMPTON MARVEL.

never " got " a real flyer, although he was used a great
deal at stud. Marsden Rush was, I think, the best he
ever sired, and he was one of the gamest dogs within my
memory. At one time he was in the same kennel as
Ch. Clonmel Marvel, and I have a very vivid recollection
of an argument started by old Clip as to who had the
right to fetch my walking stick from the Thames, and I
very nearly lost all three. They were woeful sights when
at last we got them on shore, and, as a result, Marvel
and Rush were in hospital for weeks after.

Very romantic was the history of Marvel, over whom
I and my partner have had many debates. He was bred
by a farmer, Mr. F. C. Brown, of Warfield, Berks.,
who, I believe, bought his dam from Mr. H. M. Bryans.
He, with the writer, was an exhibitor at a small show at
Lewisham. At this same show a Mr. C. Russell was
also showing a neat Terrier-like customer in a dog called
Clipper, who was awarded a second prize to my own dog,
Crack Royal, Marvel's dam, Cholmondeley Mona, re-
ceiving third. Mr. Brown was keen to use Crack Royal,
but, fortunately for myself, as time proved, I was
obdurate in the matter of fees, and at last Clipper was
fixed upon, the grand result being, in course of time, Ch.
Clonmel Marvel. I am perfectly assured that, had
Crack Royal been fixed up, there would have been
no Marvel. This Clipper has often been confounded with another son of old Clip, viz., Clipper
'94, and in the United States has generally had the
credit of getting Marvel, the breeding on the dam's side
being quite different. However, to my muttons. Mona
threw a litter of nine, and at seven months old Mr.
Brown decided to give Warfield Victor, as he was named
then, a run, but, unfortunately for himself, selected a
£3 Selling class at a small show at Reading for his
maiden effort, and he was awarded a *second* prize. I
have often marvelled why my friend, Mr. Frank Butler,

whose knowledge of a broken-haired Terrier is, I think, equal to that of any other fancier in this country, should have placed what was conceded to be a very moderate Bedlington Terrier over Marvel. The explanation, and a perfectly proper one, was that this dog utterly refused to show. The owner of the winner, Mr. J. J. Holgate, whose razor-like keenness of perception where a "pick-up" is concerned has passed into a proverb, very quickly negotiated the claiming clause, to his own immense profit, and to the chagrin of Victor's owner, who, as is not seldom the case, wished to retain possession when he found that his estimate of the dog was very far out. In twenty-four hours Mr. Royston Mills and myself had an imperative summons to come to Surbiton and buy the best Airedale alive. We had in the past seen so very many "best alives" that our frame of mind leaned strongly to the pessimistic. Five minutes, however, sufficed to change the ownership, for the largest cheque ever written in this country for an Airedale, and never was a better investment made, for after one or two setbacks, Marvel downed every dog or bitch in the strongest competition, frequently being the recipient of cups for best dog in show. He put up the record of eighteen successive championships, and, like so many of the cream of the breed, was exported to the United States. His sale was a very sensational one and the price was a huge one, and it was an immense satisfaction to fanciers in this country that his career out there was one long chapter of success. He was a great sportsman and, I think, the most lovable dog I ever remember. I have a vivid recollection of feeling very miserable and downhearted when I saw him for the last time on board the liner. With him went Ch. Clonmel Sensation and Clonmel Veracity, who both, with Marvel, helped the breed along very much. Mr. J. L. Lorillard, Arden, was the plucky purchaser, and he had no cause to regret his

CH. DUMBARTON LASS.

enterprise. He most surely laid the foundation-stone to the Airedale's meteoric leap to the American public's favour, a popularity that, for enthusiasm and numbers, has outstripped that of the Old Country.

About this time, at a small show at Woolwich, another gem was unearthed by Mr. A. E. Jennings, Dumbarton Lass being benched at this show and catalogued at twenty-five pounds. Mr. Fred Gresham, the judge, in spite of her very rough condition of coat, very quickly picked her out from amongst the ruck, and awarded her some first prizes. She was quickly claimed by Mr. Jennings, and for two or three seasons she was well-nigh invincible. She was bred by Capt. Baird Smith, who certainly entertained an angel unawares in this glorious bitch. Barring her coat and colour she was peerless. There was a strong suggestion of the bar sinister in her pedigree, but my own conviction has always been that she was bred true enough, and this is strengthened by the many good sons and daughters she has left behind her. On the break-up of Mr. Jennings's very powerful kennel, she, with the majority of her kennel mates, came into the possession of Mr. Stuart Noble. This well-known fancier up to that time had had little opportunity to indulge what, to him, amounted to a passion for the Airedale, but when at last business cares released him, he took the occasion by both hands, and for a time possessed a team which at that period had never been equalled in one kennel. What stirring memories of strenuous battles are aroused by the names of that famous bitch and Ch. Master Briar, Ch. Arthington Tinner, and Briarwood (who never was, but ought to have been, a champion).

The happenings were highly sensational at this time, and fears were entertained that a " corner " was projected, but these fears were baseless, and this, for the time, great kennel was dispersed over the face of the

c

earth, not through any diminution of enthusiasm on Mr.
Noble's part, but through sheer unmerited misfortune.
Lass found a home in the kennel of Mr. Jos. A.
Laurin, of Montreal, and that is equivalent to saying
that the " best time " that genial fancier could possibly
give Kitty was hers. Somewhere about 1896 a small
coterie of breeders was established at Bath and Chippenham. One of these gentlemen, Mr. Fred. Orledge, was
the first to astonish the Airedale world with the production of the aforementioned Briarwood, benched for
the first time at St. Pancras Show, London. He took
all Airedale hearts by storm. Mr. Hunter Johnston
was the lucky individual to become the owner of this
superlatively grand puppy at this show, and that veteran
fancier, whose knowledge of the breed was then, and
perhaps is now, equal to that of any breeder, however
eminent, would be the first to admit that Briarwood
was one of the finest investments he ever handled,
out of one of the most amazingly consistent winner
producers within my memory, Bath Lady, and a tap root
for three-quarters of the front rankers of to-day. Hynd-
man Briar was the sire, a son of Willow Nut, but, in my
judgment, an infinitely superior Terrier. But yet, despite
great chances, he failed utterly and lamentably in getting
anything near first-class, except by the alliance with this
remarkable matron. So that breeders of this line of blood
will be wise in their generation in putting their money
on the bitch side of the house. This is amply proved, because, when put to Ch. Clonmel Marvel, the result was
winners, and the same result when allied to Ch. Master
Briar was evolved.

Ch. Clonmel Kitty was the next that this prolific gold
mine produced. She was bought by the writer for four
pounds, and afterwards sold for very many times that
figure. I have never seen a more thoroughly charming
animal than old Kitty. She is still alive and looks like

CH. TONE JERRY, CH. TONE CRACK, CH. TONE REGENT,
THE CHAMPIONS FROM THE TONE KENNELS.

a two-year-old, and when I saw her last, was as gay and debonair as a puppy. To Mr. G. H. Elder belongs the absolute credit of making this bitch a champion. There was also Chippenham Daisy, Rex per Saltum — the latter bred by Mr. Pounds — Clonmel Veracity, who, up to that, was far and away the best bitch out, but was a vile shower, and never did get her deserts in consequence. It was then that Mr. Marshall Lee, who will always be gratefully remembered by the writer for his whole-hearted assistance in keeping an even keel for the South of England Airedale Terrier Club. The proper type of president—a worker and not a worrier. Every emergency found him ready with just that tactful aid that a badgered hon. secretary is now and again just in need of. Mr. Lee conceived the idea that Master Briar, being on finer lines, would just give that touch of quality which, with the exception of Clonmel Kitty, all the progeny of Bath Lady lacked. It was really a brilliant inspiration, and the alliance was justified by the production of Walton Victory, who in a great many ways was an absolute flyer— such ribs, bone and hindquarters, a head that the hypercritical perhaps would call doggy, all in all. She was fit to rank with the select band within the doggy valhalla whom we cherish as our ideals in the realms of our fancy. Miss Arnold, now Mrs. Baker, had a decided penchant for this blood, and her team of Burlys were, at this time, formidable at the Southern shows.

Another Terrier with undeniable claims to notice in a book that claims to be historical was very successful about this time, chiefly in the South of England—Broadlands Bunkum. He emanated from a kennel that was afterwards destined to become famous by the home production of Ch. Broadlands Bashful and Ch. Broadlands Royal Descendant. Bunkum never was a favourite

of mine, although it is only fair to say that a great
number of people considered him in the first flight; but
Bashful was a glorious Airedale, perfect in make and
shape, and the most marvellous front, legs, and feet, combined with great bone, I ever saw. Her coat was her
trouble. This I expect she inherited from her dam,
Broadlands Burelle, a rare sort of brood bitch. I suppose
Bashful was the best dog or bitch that Briarwood ever
sired, and she ranks with the best bitch I have ever seen.
She also put up a great record in the way of championships; I forget the number. Studholme Sherry had a
meteoric career in this year 1896. He did not last in
skull as well as could be wished, but those fanciers who
may have lines of that blood in their kennel can rest
assured that he was a very high-class Terrier, and built
on the most alluring lines of Terrier make and shape,
with a grand head, beautiful ears, and a very fetching
front. I know Mr. Emil Sachse was very proud of him;
he was by Briar Test, out of Red Linnet, right back to
the grand coloured and coated Rustic Rushlight. I have
often regretted that our own kennel had not the nous to
keep Marsden Rush. Given a fair chance, I am absolutely
convinced that this dog would have left an indelible mark
upon the breed in everything that counts for coat, colour,
eye and soundness. I rather think that Rush is now
revelling in the lovely climate of Ceylon.

A nailing good puppy that came out about this time
was Accrington Rough. I don't think in all my ex-
periences I have ever seen a grander made one, and his
neck and shoulders were phenomenally good. He was
exported rather early in his show life to Australia by the
Rock Ferry firm, Messrs. Baines and Dodwell, who were
going very strong in the breed at this time. In this connection I was informed by an old Airedale fancier who was
over here for a trip (Mr. S. W. Duncan, of Adelaide),
that Rough had sired a large number of average stock, but

E. R. L. HOSKINS.

of course his chances were few of getting the right sort of bitch.

The great Tone kennel at Taunton had a great say in the distribution of the prize list at this period with Ch. Tone Jerry, a gentleman of a Terrier, very sound, and absolutely without fluff. I had expected this dog to leave a great mark upon the breed, but somehow, probably through lack of opportunity, no really great puppy came by alliance with Jerry. Ch. Tone Crack was another who in the useful argot of the ring "came too soon." A sturdily built Terrier, well boned and sound coated, he was, I think, seldom beaten, but retired rather early. A contemporary of the last named dog, Ch. Rock Salt, over whom there was a tremendous difference of opinion, started his show career at Derby, under Mr. Midgley Marsden; a raw unfurnished puppy he yet looked like making a name. Such promise was amply borne out in course of time. When fully furnished he beat, bar Ch. Clonmel Monarch, all the dogs in the country. He never was a prime favourite of the writer's, as I always thought him lacking in true Terrier character, and I can only remember one really good class puppy by him. The New King, who preceded Monarch to America, was a very sound, good dog, who required " no aids." This dog has sired a large number of high-class stock in that country, and has himself qualified for an American championship. If I might give a paddock "snip" to our cousins I would say, put your Monarch bitches to the New King, and the result will, I am persuaded, be very gratifying.

The first of a celebrated line of " Masters " came out at Cheltenham, and succeeded in reaching championship honours there; a very sound dog, wonderful coat and colour, but decidedly short and plain in head. He was a scion of those two devoted old kennel mates, Ch. Clonmel Marvel and Ch. Clonmel Kitty, and he inherited to the full all their high qualities of gameness and good sense.

Clonmel Gamecock had a great time while he lasted. He was the result of an alliance with Marvel and a Clip bitch, Clonmel Busy, and this was the only time that the Clip strain had failed to assert itself in the matter of dark eyes. I never could stand Gamecock's lamps. Like his rival, Ch. Rock Salt, he lacked Terrier character, and, as I fully anticipated, has done nothing for the breed.

Just at this time I had the high privilege of seeing an absolute wonder at six months old in Ch. Clonmel Monarch, before, of course, he bore that proud title. His breeder, Mr. Berkinshaw Smith, who even at that time had little to learn from anybody about an Airedale, knew what he had got, and was not to be persuaded to part. However, circumstances over which the most far-seeing are powerless to guard against, compelled Mr. Smith to part with his favourite. Myself and partner were duly advised, and the great Monarch was exchanged for Clonmel gold. Never have I in my life seen a head so magnificently shaped, such power and expression, and the very quintessence of Terrier fire. I am perhaps wrong in saying '' never,'' as I have before me as I write the living counterpart; but that, as Rudyard Kipling would say, is another story. In body shape he was ultra grand, legs like pillars, and sound as a bell of brass all over. Faults! Well, there are spots on the sun; his coat, which was pig bristle in texture, had that peculiar curl which those with knowledge usually associate with hardness, and which invariably carries no fluff. Judges vied with each other in heaping their judicial favours upon this wonderful dog, and he became a champion in double quick time. He was benched for the first time at Leicester, but his immaturity just stopped him from reaching the highest honours, and he was placed reserve to Ch. Rock Salt, who was looking his very best on that day. I well remember some of our oldest Terrier judges while conceding Monarch to be in some ways great, yet

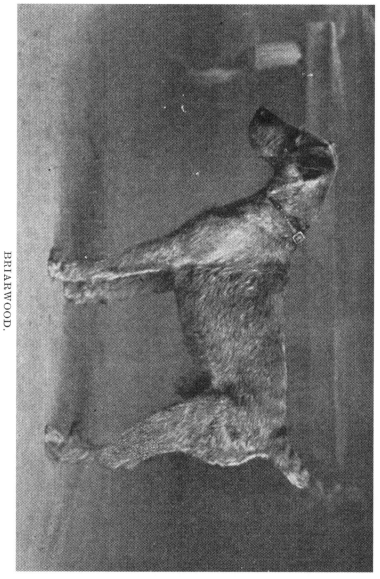

BRIARWOOD.

they thought him too bitchy; but the critics were confounded on his next appearance. In the interim he had come along splendidly, and his certificate was unspoiled after Leicester by defeat in his classes and at the Alexandra Palace. After winning the championship from his sire he put up the greatest performance possible for any dog of any breed by winning the Midland Counties challenge cup from ten other champions, under possibly a triumvirate of the most famous all-round judges in the world.

I well remember that my dear old friend, the late Herbert Jones, who had that wonderful bitch, Babette of Moreton, who was without a shadow of doubt the best smooth Collie ever bred, and she was amongst Monarch's victims, so the strength of the competition may easily be imagined—poor Herbert Jones, with that courtly courtesy which always distinguished him in all affairs, was the first to offer his congratulations and so, within a stone's throw of where this wonderful Terrier was born, he was covering himself with canine glory. Monarch is ever a fascinating theme upon which I have often descanted since his export to Philadelphia. Another victory, of which my partner and myself were very proud, was the winning of the coveted gold medal at Otley. It was at this show that Monarch took such a wide and spacious revenge on his Leicester conqueror. We have many times won the gold medal at this Airedale function, but the pleasure of Monarch's success will ever taste the sweetest, gained as it was under one of the finest Terrier judges in this country, and who in addition bears an international reputation for knowledge and integrity. Mr. F. M. Jowett, even after this momentous judgment, in crisp significant sentence, with straight Yorkshire doric eloquence, said, " He absolutely fills the bill "; and this dictum was well-nigh unanimously endorsed by the fancy. Monarch piled Pelion upon Ossa after this, and never

looked back. His last appearance before an Aireda'e
public, which, rightly or wrongly, had gone wild over
him, was made at Cruft's previous to his exportation to
the United States. As it happened, it was as successful
a farewell as all farewells should be. Ch. Tone Masterpiece was the runner-up, and afterwards Monarch beat
Ch. Broadlands Bashful for a mixed special. I feel
vividly even now the poignant grief with which I parted
with this favourite of the ring, and it is an absolute fact
that had Mr. E. Royston Mills not been abroad at the
time Monarch never would have left this country, to our
own immense gain, aye, and to the fancy's immense gain,
but to America's irreparable loss. As brilliant a performer as he was on the bench, he has proved to de-
monstration his power as a stud force in both countries,
though not two years old at the time of his expatriation.
The following is the truly remarkable tally of his
successful sons and daughters:—Ch. Clonmel Bed Rock,
Tone Regent, Broadlands Royal Descendant, Clonmel
Coronation, Tone Regent, Clonmel Majesty (a shy lady,
but when showing I have never seen a much
better specimen), Strathallan Solace, poor unfortunate
Claverhouse Enchantress (the mother of champions),
and a lot of other grand ones, who have left an
indelible mark upon the breed. · The sale caused an
immense sensation at the time, and we were freely
criticised for parting with a dog that would have set
the type for all time; but every kennel has the
right to manage its own affairs as it thinks fit. If one
thing is certain more than anything else in the history
of the breed, it is that our great sensational sales of
young champions to the United States at various times
helped largely, and even tremendously, to popularise the
Airedale in both countries, and the fancier with a small
stock shared in the boom equally with the large establishments.

CH. BROADLANDS BASHFUL.

The sportsmanship of selling "good-old-have-beens" to the foreign markets is debatable, but it is to be remembered that all our great sales in every case were of young, vigorous dogs and bitches who were top notchers in this country, and they never failed to get the same after exportation to America.

Clonmel Marvel never tasted the bitterness of defeat until he met his Waterloo in Philadelphia. His grand son, Monarch, was his conqueror. Monarch, I think, was never beaten in that country, and George Raper, after judging him in New York, said that he could down the lot in this country also.

A dog came out at the Kennel Club Show in 1900. His merits were appraised at the value of v.h.c., but he was in good company, for on the same mark came Ch. Master Briar. It is certainly only fair to Mr. Pendlebury, who officiated on this tragic occasion, to say that both Terriers were dead out of form, and this, doubtless, influenced this famous Welsh Terrier judge and exhibitor in turning them down. For after all, dog shows are for the proper encouragement of form and condition as well as purely fancy points, and Mr. Pendlebury proved himself the possessor of great pluck, and is to be commended for the display of that admirable quality, without which no judge can be truly great.

In very different guise, however, Tone Masterpiece made his next appearance, and a successful one. He was a Terrier from stem to stern, full of fire—the divine spark, if I may say so, the hall-mark of nearly every great Terrier within my memory—eyes that glowed with correct Terrier character, true and straight all round, a real "swell," whichever way you looked at him. No dog that I wot of had fairer claims to the proud title of champion, which, however, was long in coming. Had he been gifted with his sire's remarkable strength of jaw,

I don't suppose he would ever have been beaten. However, after a stormy career here, where he had more ups and downs than he deserved, he joined the distinguished band of remarkable Terriers already domiciled in the land of the Stars and Stripes, where he had a great time at the head of the prize list, and was seldom beaten. His son, Clonmel Floriform, out of that good old slave, Clonmel Caramel, downed him at New York, under George Raper.

Always a very much under-rated Terrier was the same Floriform. Given a little more length of head and a sounder coat, and he could top the competition in any country. Two championships fell to him in England, and I rather fancy that he qualified for the full title of champion in the United States. A kennel fight, which left him minus one of his ears, cut short his bench career. He sired out there the best bitch of 1904 in Ingaflora, a great winner since. The sensational Bank House Guest, and numerous minor lights, who did their fair share of winning about that time, also claimed him as their sire.

A greater Terrier than Floriform, and one who had a much more distinguished career, was Ch. Legrams Prince. He made his debut under one of the keenest and strongest supporters the fancy ever had, Mr. Harold Mitchell, of Birmingham. Prince was a raw, immature sort of dog, but with rare promise for the future, which, as the books of the breed will tell us, he amply fulfilled. Ch. Clonmel Bed Rock was his conqueror on this occasion, but of this Terrier more anon. I don't think that Prince came out again until Cruft's, 1902, where he literally swept the decks from Open to Puppy class, and never were victories better deserved. He was a perfect picture of hard, beautiful form, showing like a hackney, and he spreadeagled the field. I had myself at that time a very useful performer in the ring in Clonmel Warlock, and

CH. MASTER BRIAR.

fancied myself mighty for first honours until I caught sight of Legrams Prince. My feelings then were much like Bret Harte's politician:—

> "Just then a chunk of brick
> Struck him on the jaw,
> And the subsequent proceedings,
> Interested him no more."

After this show Prince had a.clean march through to full championship. Absolutely the type we all aim at, in his day he was quite entitled to rank amongst the best. His final performance was the capturing of that little bit of gold, the ambition of thousands of true fanciers' hearts, the gold medal of Otley. I was the adjudicator, and he won with consummate ease. A rheumatic affection of one of his forelegs stopped this great dog in his prime. I had a commission to buy him for a South African fancier after he had retired from the ring. The price was fixed, and I got his owner to the parting pitch, but calm reflections found Mr. Hoskins utterly unable to part with his pal, and a large sum of money had to be forfeited. Sportsmanship of this sort is sufficiently rare, and it is well worth recording.

Another son of Monarch who created no end of stir in this year was Bandolero. He won a few minor prizes behind Legrams Prince at this show, and gave ample promise of future eminence with maturity. He was a long time, however, in properly furnishing; in fact, it may be said that he never did furnish like some winners I know. He probably suffered with his liver. Mr. Arthur Maxwell took an immense fancy to this Terrier at Manchester in 1903, and he was awarded three firsts and the championship over all the best dogs of the day. I always had a great penchant for Bandolero, and tried hard to buy him at Cruft's, but Mr. Palk would not part. However, this noted Terrier went on the down line after Manchester. He never was benched in anything like good form, and that was the sole reason for his non-success. He met with a particularly sad end at Bournemouth. Benched at that show, he ran second to Clonmel St. Windeline.

At this same show was a plausible sort of puppy catalogued at five pounds, which was claimed by Mr. Roberts, a veterinary surgeon to the show, and a brother-in-law of Mr. Royston Mills, hence, no doubt, his eye for an Airedale. Bandolero's owner was also very sweet on the Selling puppy, but was too late to claim. He, however, not to be baulked, and after a deal of negotiation, to everybody's amazement, not unmingled with amusement, made an *even* swop of Bandolero for the aforesaid puppy. The poor dog, however, was not destined to become what he, without an atom of doubt, deserved to become, a champion. Two days after the show, while on the golf links of that favourite resort, he was stung by a wasp, and was found dead four days later in a wood. He deserved a better fate, for, if fit enough, he would undoubtedly have beaten the front-rankers. A contemporary of the last-named, Ch. Wombwell Rattler, was fairly successful, and was often leading from some of the best dogs of the day. His chief " out " was his coat, which never was orthodox, but withal a sound, good Airedale. Some of his good qualities he very evidently must have transmitted to his son, Jurgens De Wet, who, under a judge of Mr. A. Clarkson's judicial eminence, obtained the championship at Edinburgh, and was promptly claimed by Mr. Geo. Thomas, who has a reputation on both sides of the Atlantic, so that it is easy to gather that this dog, like his celebrated namesake, must have been a good one, and under the name of York the Conqueror he pretty well beat the best in the United States.

Ch. Tone Regent, another debutant of that historical period, by *Ch. Clonmel Monarch ex Tone Victoria*, had a great time amongst the best. He resembles his dam very

CH. CROMPTON PERFORMER.

greatly, a wonderfully timbered dog, very harsh coat, a very long head, and a grand natural coat and colour. His eyes were light and ears not clever, but judge him all in all, he was worthy to rank in the select gallery of celebrities.

Walton Victory, bred by the then President of the South of England Airedale Terrier Club, Mr. Marshall Lee, sire Ch. Master Briar, dam, the gold mine, Bath Lady, was perhaps unlucky not to have secured her final championship. She was awarded two, one at Liverpool for best dog or bitch, and one at Birmingham. At the last-named show she beat a nailing good lot of bitches, and the verdict hung in suspense a long time. Finally, she won by a narrow margin, closely followed by Gains-borough Duchess and Rock Ferry Vixen. Duchess was a pick-up, a rare good sort, but rather doggy in head, and her shoulders were decidedly loose. Rock Ferry Vixen, on the other hand, had splendid shoulders, rare legs and feet, a right down good jacket; a real good Terrier, but on the coarse side. A bitch of rather opposite type and structure to the last-named three, Ch. Delph Girl, came out at Otley in 1902. I thought her a well-made one, with fine head and expression and a good black coat. I gave her some first prizes, but hardly thought her first class. She was too Welsh in type to altogether fill my eye. However, she furnished a full-blown champion, and had quite a successful show life in the United States. Two Terriers came out in 1901 who were destined to play a tremendous part in the future history of the breed, Claverhouse Enchantress, by Ch. Clonmel Monarch, ex Clonmel Winifreda. She won a few first prizes, and was always in the money, but it was as a matron that she was to become famous. I sold her to Mrs. Cuthell at six months, with a service to a dog I was to select. I believe that this celebrated bitch was the first Airedale that Mrs. Cuthell ever owned, so that it

was a case of novice's luck again. Like most carefully bred
stock, Enchantress had the priceless faculty of throwing
champions. The first, Dumbarton Sceptre, was benched for
the first time at Cruft's. She failed to meet the judicial
eye with distinction. I liked her myself exceedingly, and
offered to buy, but failed to deal; however, I got a
promise of first refusal, with which I had to be content.
The promise was loyally kept by Mrs. Cuthell, for when
Mr. Theo. Kershaw wired an offer for Witch, as she then
was named, Mrs. Cuthell telegraphed to me at Manchester putting the bitch at such a price that I would
have clinched the matter instantly, but, tragically enough,
I had left for home, being right down ill, and I did not
receive the wire for days afterwards, which was real bad
luck. Still, there was a great consolation in the knowledge that this magnificent specimen was in the right
hands to do her justice. She was easily the best Airedale
benched at this, and how Mr. J. R. Cooper, who even at
this time owned some eminent dogs, came to miss this
superlatively beautiful bitch, is a marvel to the knowing
ones who were present. She seemed to the ringsiders to
have stood clean away from the opposition. Still, judges
are only human, and therefore liable like the rest of us
to err. I don't think that Sceptre was ever beaten after
she changed hands. She had a wonderful career, and
finally went to that land where all England's Airedale
" good goods " go to. Mr. Theo. Offerman was the lucky
man, and I am convinced that he never regretted becom-
ing the possessor of one of the best bitches of the decade.
A litter brother of the above-mentioned bitch,
Claverhouse Sorcerer, did not " last " like his celebrated
relative. He, however, had his points, and at eight
months old was quite as good, but his shoulders went a
little and his skull thickened; still, when he left this
country he was quite a Terrier of class. I had in the
meantime arranged with the owner of Enchantress to take

STRATHALAN SOLACE.

the bitch on breeding terms, the sire I selected being Ch. Master Briar. The result, as all the Airedale world knows, was Ch. Mistress Royal, the most remarkable bitch within my memory. In addition to winning championship after championship in her own classes, she has many times been in the front rank in the very hottest variety classes, and has in this way beaten most champions of other breeds in open competition. I have never seen a better specimen, and I never expect to. A litter brother, who would without a shadow of doubt have been in course of time a celebrity, joined the great majority when just furnishing for high competition. Before the litter was born Mrs. Cuthell found that she could not possibly do without Enchantress at home, and the breeding arrangement was mutually broken. In course of time I had the felicity of paying a very large sum of money for Mistress Royal, and a stiff figure also for a dog puppy. Enchantress was bred to her son, Sorcerer, after this, but picked up some poison, and died. A heavy loss to her owner and a still greater loss to the breed; I would myself have given a great deal of money for her. Her brother, Strathallan Solace, was a '' gift horse '' to Miss Kennedy, but he certainly lacked the luck that is usually associated with gift horses. He had done a great deal of winning, but he was mostly under-rated, because of his lack of fire when in the ring. Although one of the gamest dogs possible, as a sire he was not nearly so much used as he deserved, and I have often begged fanciers to put their hopes to him. Cherry Royal and Strathallan Solitaire were both by Solace, and I am game to prophesy that those lucky individuals who have in their kennels representatives of this particular line of prepotent blood will have immense cause for congratulation in the near future. Gipsy Countess, who was just one notch short of being a full champion, came out in 1901. I made her the best bitch at Otley, and up to 1902 she had done a great deal of winning. I was certainly enamoured of her as being one of the most stylish Airedales possible to conceive, having a rare good body and coat. She was just short of length from eye to nose, else I don't suppose she ever would have been beaten. Ch. Clonmel Bed Rock came out at Manchester, under Mr. A. Clarkson, and won all he was entered for. His nearest opponent was Briar Rocket, and the judge, in an interesting and clever report in the " Kennel Gazette," explained that Bed Rock won on maturity, but if he had to choose which to take home he would choose the " firework." What an exceedingly bad shot this eminent judge would have made history amply proves; but even " Homer used to nod " sometimes. Ch. Broadlands Royal Descendant was very close on the above-named Terrier some time after this, although he never actually got his head in front. Descendant had the advantage in liberty, but Bed Rock scored decisively in legs and feet, bone, skull, and hindquarters.

I remember after coming home from Edinburgh I imparted the information to the partners of Royal Descendant, that Bed Rock had been to his last show in England, and was off to the States. Mr. Clarkson then very reasonably guessed that they would win their championship at Cruft's. My own view then expressed, which really proved almost inspired, was that I could race Descendant with an unshown puppy, but that another puppy, Legrams Prince, would lick us both, and the placings were: Legrams Prince first, Descendant second, Clonmel Warlock third, Geo. Raper judging. Clonmel Coronation had just previously left the country, after having a great time here, and was soon after joined by Bed Rock. In this brace of Terriers, when shown in proper form, Mr. Foxhall Keen had something of which any fancier should be proud.

In this article I am desirous of writing only of those

CH. BROADLANDS ROYAL DESCENDANT.

Terriers who have left these shores for ever; or of those dogs which have been retired from the show benches by death or other causes. It would be invidious to compare the dogs of to-day in a book of this sort. I have thought that by an impartial review of past celebrities, especially those who have left their mark upon the breed by reproduction, it would be a great aid to the breeder to know where the different pillars of our stud book failed and where they excelled. History is therefore exceedingly valuable as an object lesson to that most deserving of all mortals, the scientific breeder.

CHAPTER II.

Description and Standard of the Airedale Terrier.

Long, with flat skull, but not too broad between the ears, narrowing slightly to the eyes, free from wrinkle; stop hardly visible and cheeks free from fulness; jaw deep and powerful, well filled up before the eyes; lips tight; ears V-shaped, with a side carriage, small but not out of proportion to the size of the dog; the nose black; the eyes small and dark in colour, not prominent, and full of Terrier expression, with teeth strong and level; the neck should be of moderate length and thickness, gradually widening towards the shoulders, and free from throatiness. Shoulders and chest: shoulders long and sloping well into the back; shoulder blades flat, chest deep, but not broad; body and back short, strong and straight; ribs well sprung; hindquarters strong and muscular, with no drop; hocks well let down; the tail set on high and carried gaily, but not curled over the back. Legs and feet: legs perfectly straight, with plenty of bone; feet small and round, with good depth of pad; coat, hard and wiry, and not so long as to appear ragged; it should be also straight and close, covering the dog well over the body and legs. Colour: the head and ears, with the exception of dark markings on each side of the skull, should be tan, the ears being of a darker shade than the rest, the legs up to the thighs and elbows being tan; the body black or dark grizzle. Size: dogs 40lb. to 45lb. weight; bitches slightly less.

Scale of points—head 5, eye 5, colour 10, ears 5, body, loins and hindquarters 20, jaw 10, nose 5, teeth 5, legs and feet 10, neck and shoulders 10, coat 15; total, 100.

CH. ARTHINGTON TINNER.

In a mind's picture of an ideal Airedale garnered from
the above scale of points, the eye first takes in a head,
long and classically formed, the skull perfectly flat and
entirely without cheek, not too much width between; the
beautifully small ears, which are carried high and close
to the cheek, surmount a pair of eyes full of intelligence
and fire, dark in colour, and small in comparison to the
size of dog; stop hardly visible. A strong square
muzzle, jaw very powerful, filled right up before the eyes
by bone under the eye, muzzle covered with whiskers of
sound colour, not linty, big black nose, beneath which
should be a set of white even teeth. The head should now
be set on a long, graceful neck, which will arch into the
sloping shoulders. Facing your ideal—the forelegs as
straight as iron bars, their thick flat bone covered with
hard tan hair, inside and out, right down to the small,
round cat feet. He stands for all his weight as lightly as
a deer, with no symptom of weakness at the pastern
joints; on a broadside view the first impression is one of
sturdy, squareness combined with symmetry. From
shoulder to rump the back is perfectly level, and meets
the tail absolutely erect, flashing challenges to all
comers; the breadth of the hindquarters more than
balanced by the depth of brisket and the grandly sprung
ribs, the heart having ample room for play; the coat
crisp and hard to the touch, with never a curl or wave in
its beautiful black or grizzle, but with an oily undercoat
beneath which is impervious to the vagaries of any
climate. If the picture absolutely fills your eye, the
whole effect should be that of a muscular, active, fairly
cobby Terrier, without a suspicion of legginess and undue
length of barrel. See him galloping—he moves like a
racehorse, his every movement the poetry of motion, with
nose well to the ground in search of his quarry; he looks
what he is, a gentleman and a workman. From the fore-
going, the seeker after hidden truths should be able to

form a fairly accurate idea of the general appearance of a classic Airedale, and by careful comparison to distinguish the more obvious " outs " of a bad one, but only actual experience can teach him the great lesson of differentiation in the closer shades of the plausible and the merely moderate, and of the real top notcher and the flat catcher. Then, as his keen powers of analysis mature, so will he find it a fascinating study to reason out for himself the why and the wherefore of the different placings by the various " Solons " who adjudicate upon the breed. Only by this means will the novice attain the idea of the general conformation and type to breed to, and during his novitiate he will store up an enormous variety of information and, perhaps, appraise at something near a proper valuation the many widely divergent opinions and theories of canine experts, who, like other members of the community, are not invariably unanimous.

A certain class of breeder, who prefer undue measure for money, will go for size above every other point ; others go " potty " over colour and bone ; and I am bound to state that the majority judge the dog by its head alone—most fatal of all blunders. It is useless for anyone to keep on breeding unless they have—or can carefully cultivate—the sense of proportion. Keen and thorough study of the points laid down here, and their relative values, together with a carefully cultivated eye for the " altogether," is the surest way to build up and maintain a strain which is the eternal ambition of every budding fancier.

BANDOLERO.

CHAPTER III.

How to Breed Exhibition Specimens.

The unexpressed desire of every fancier's heart on observing the winning career of a great champion, whom, rightly or wrongly, he instinctively chooses as his ideal, is to own or breed such a one. For the same reason that the philosopher cynically said, that fleas were necessary to the dog to help him to forget that he was a dog, so are hobbies and pastimes given to us that we should not dwell too much on matters that are unbalancing to the mind.

It is, of course, quite an elementary matter for a rich man, by the simple process of cheque signing, to become possessed of a champion dog of the day; or it sometimes happens that the comparative neophyte breeds one by a fluke. The flukes in breeding live stock have been a fascinating wonder to the scientist for ages. Breeders of to-day are lucky in their generation. They have a bedrock of ascertained facts to work upon which was necessarily denied to the pioneers. Type, that bugbear of all breeds, at any rate in Airedales, is now fixed definitely, so that the theory path, beset as it was with almost insurmountable obstacles, which was the common lot of the breeders of ten years ago, is now fairly smooth, and the patient striver after perfection, if his enthusiasm will only hold out, will find himself in the promised land where champions and typical specimens are as thick as leaves at the fall in Vallambrosa.

There are simple rules in every game or hobby by which alone it is possible to secure the best results. The first rule should be to avoid, as you would the pestilence, the advertising windbag, who generally buys to sell, and is utterly ignorant of the first rules of proper mating. By this I must not be taken to mean that the starter should invariably go to the large breeding establishments for his breeding stock. There are hundreds of breeders in this country who keep only one or two bitches from whom carefully-bred specimens may be acquired. The first step, therefore, to be taken is the acquirement of a sound, healthy bitch.. The closer she can compare to the standard, as laid down in these pages, the surer the ultimate success will be. Carefully to fix on one of the correct type is the first desideratum : that the ears should be small and correctly carried, and, above all, the eyes dark and Terrier-like. These are absolute essentials. Bone, coat, and contour may be pretty well reckoned as a certainty from the carefully-selected stud dog. More failures have been registered by novice breeders taking as their text in buying the future matron the shibboleths of big, roomy, and great boned bitches. All three points are purely relative, and have no inherent virtue of their own alone. Above all things, stick to type, and with ordinary luck success is assured.

A young maiden bitch is much the best investment, and, providing she has fairly well matured, the first heat in my own experience has shown the best results. The truest economy is to pay a fair price for the right article, a rule that the " heads " of every profession teach. An instance may fairly be given in Claverhouse Enchantress, bought for £20. She turned out two champions, and would, had she lived, have turned out others. Clonmel St. Windeline, much about the same price, also threw two champions, and in all probability another puppy that will be a champion before these lines are in print. Tone Betty, the mother of Ch. Tone Chief, Bath Lady, and hosts of others. And now, in the choice of a suitable mate, the owner should use all the force of his intellect, and, if possible, the advice and assistance of

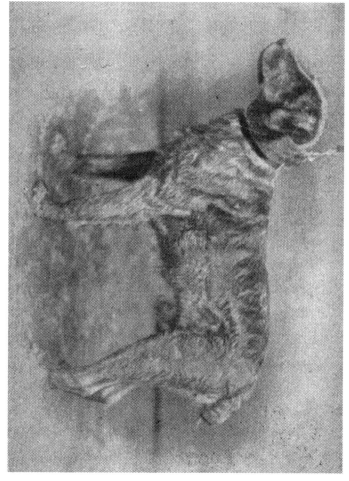

CH. WHARFEDALE RUSH.

any eminent breeder who may be willing, and most of them are so willing, men who have made the science of reproduction a life-long study. The terms prepotency, variability, heredity, and atavism must be the elementary texts upon which he will base the groundwork of his breeding efforts. Each factor will in its turn have important bearings from time to time. By prepotency we mean the power inherent in certain individuals of both sexes of stamping certain members of the family with certain important characteristics, no matter how various in points or blood their partners may be. Variability is the striking dissimilarity in appearance, or in personal characteristics of almost every puppy in the litter. Heredity is the stamping of the character and points of parents to their puppies. The next is of the most vital importance in a breed whose mixed ancestry is by no means remote. Atavism is the tendency of all animals to throw back to their ancestors. The first point in the full grasping of these terms is to remember that the dog is the offspring of the whole line of blood from generations, and not merely the result of the alliance of his sire and dam.

The best basis to work upon is to take it that the sire and dam between them contribute one-half of the inherited characteristics, and the four grand-parents would contribute another quarter. It will be readily conceded that success would therefore in a great measure depend upon the breeder being as far as possible conversant with the faults and virtues of both sire and dam and their back blood, with its characteristics as far back as possible. It is a vexed question as to how far we should inbreed for the purpose of stamping some important point. My own opinion, based upon experience as varied and as wide as most breeders', is that for a proper regard to the stamina of the breed, the conscientious fancier for every once he breeds in should

preserve the balance as far as may be by breeding twice
out. All these matters carefully weighed and digested
by the beginner, we come back now to the foundation of
a successful kennel. The breeder should certainly not
part with any of his pups before the age of five months,
unless there are some obviously unfit by constitution or
too much white on the toes, or that they are absolutely
smooth, with no promise of whiskers on the face. At
five or six months old the best policy to pursue is to keep
for himself the most promising dog and the most
promising bitch of his first litter, and by advertising the
others for sale he should easily recoup himself for the
initial outlay of the capital. When his young bitch is of
age (and my own experience is greatly in favour of
mating bitches the first season) he will have noted where
she fails in her different qualities, and in selecting a stud
dog for her he should select a dog resembling her as
near as possible in contour, and if he possesses in a
superlative degree those excellences wherein she is
deficient, so much the more successful will the result of
the alliance be. Mayhap all this sounds formidable to
the beginner, but the enthusiast who is not easily
daunted, and possesses a sufficient fund of common-
sense and determination, combined with a genuine love of
the breed, is bound to get " right there." The apprentice-
ship is not over-long, but sufficiently arduous, and the
beginner will look back upon his failures with little
searchings of heart perhaps, but when he has acquired
that experience which alone can correct those failures,
he may look back and find many pleasant landmarks
which have brought him to the successful issue of breeding a champion, and then, maybe, when the five-guinea
stud fees come tumbling in, and two Continents are
making large demands upon his carefully-bred puppy
stock, he will find that the reward is commensurate with
his labours, and he will thus have the laugh of the slap-

JOHN G. HORROCKS.

dash brigade who, knowing nothing, and caring little for the laws of breeding, trust entirely to luck, *sans* judgment and *sans* common-sense. The management of the bitch in whelp is of the very greatest importance for six weeks after service. The bitch had better be allowed to go on her own way, as usual, but at the end of that time her condition should be carefully studied. She must be strictly guarded against any violent exercise, particularly jumping; plenty of sound food should be given three times a day, with a sufficiency of big bones with a little meat on. This will ensure the progeny having the necessary bone and muscle. A few doses of olive oil during the last two or three days of pregnancy will assure the bitch having an easy time. I have never found Airedales require assistance during the period of whelping, and they are much better left strictly alone during this operation. For a period of three days sloppy food only should be given. The mother is naturally disinclined to leave her offspring, but she should gently and firmly be compelled to take a sufficiency of exercise after the first day, or fever may supervene and upset both mother and pups. It is a debatable subject as to how many puppies a bitch should be allowed to bring up. I am strongly of opinion that in no case should the number exceed eight. And the bitch may be largely assisted in the discharge of her maternal duties if at three weeks the pups be taught to lap fresh cow's milk, and their diet afterwards increased with the addition of the finest food within my knowledge—Plasmon. I have seen some of the most astonishing results by using this food upon all sorts of puppies. I can, therefore, advise its use with the utmost confidence.

F

CHAPTER IV.

How to Rear and Manage.

At three or four days old their tails should be docked to fashion. A good rule to observe is to take about two-thirds off with a sharp knife, pressing the skin back before the cut is made. The skin will then in due course cover the slight wound. Five weeks is the best age to wean them, but before leaving their dam they should be treated once or twice for worms. This will fit them in a greater measure for their coming battle for existence. I would advise that nothing but Areca Nut should be given; it is always harmless, and generally effectual. From now dates the time that is probably the most crucial period of their lives. Not less than five meals a day should be given; absolute freedom from restraint, the utmost fresh air possible, and all the sunshine possible for them to revel in. At four months they will amply repay the breeder for all the care lavished upon them. At this age four meals a day are sufficient. At six months to seven months their teething troubles should be over, and they on the high road to future bench honours. I have for years made it a hard and fast rule that instantly the puppy reaches the age of six weeks he should be sent out to walk. I have often seen it recommended, and practised it myself, the sending out of puppies by twos; but experience has amply proved that to get a puppy really well done one to each cottage is enough. Many cottagers will take one puppy, and make him one of the family, with his box near the chimney corner. The natural consequence follows, as night follows day, that when he has romped and exercised to his heart's content, he curls up

CH. LEGRAMS PRINCE.

in great comfort in his warm corner, and thus he builds up his sturdy little frame; but when two are walked at a cottage they become burdensome to the housewife, and then get put into the garden shed out of trouble, and thus lose the comfort which is very necessary to them. At this age periodic visits should be made to make sure the pups are thriving and going the right way, and the cottager's children be encouraged to take the pup on a lead for walks. This will largely help the puppy to learn the proper ring side manner. At eight to nine months, according to individual maturity, the pups should be brought back to the kennels, and each be prepared for his future business in life. His first business, I take it, is to prove himself a sportsman. He will already have been grounded in the elementary lessons of rat-killing and river work. This, to my mind, is the most fascinating side of his many-sided character. We have a number of our Terriers now with a pack of Otter Hounds, and except for being rather too headstrong, they are right up to any Otter Hound in the pack. Their next training will be to display on the lead that debonair carriage for which this breed is famous, to induce the proper amount of fire and "go." A good plan is to have a small platform in the grounds, and if you can arrange once or twice a week for seven or eight Terriers to be showing on leather leads on this platform, it will be a great assistance by teaching them to stand on their toes, with their tails erect, ears well up, and eyes challenging comparison with each other. In every family there are puppies who for some unknown reason appear cowed, and who rarely seem to carry their tails with that gayness which is so desirable. I have never failed to effect a cure by putting such puppies in the kennel-yard with a few others; and as pluck and spirit are really contagious, they never fail within a short time to be just as courageous as an Airedale should be.

CHAPTER V.

How to Prepare for the Show Bench.

The previous chapter will have initiated the beginner into the mysteries of how puppies should be taught "to ask for the money." The future aspirant for bench honours should now be taken seriously in hand in order to get him into what is known as show form. It is fairly obvious that a young dog who has had almost perfect liberty will hardly appreciate the restraint imposed upon him by collar and lead. This, however, he will, with a little kindness, soon get used to, for a puppy for whom is undertaken the arduous labours of showing in his best bib and tucker from puppy class, with perhaps five or six intervening classes, before he reaches the real battle, the open class, it will be readily conceded that his training should be very thorough. Three hours' walking exercise on the lead is not too much, and if the person who has charge of the puppy while out takes with him a fair quantity of baked or boiled liver, and brings his charge to attention now and again, with the reward of a piece of the above delicacy, the champion in embryo will never forget it, and will in all probability while in the ring carry himself with the same dash as when on the road asking for his favourite *bonne bouche*.

All wire-haired breeds require a certain amount of attention paid to coats, generally known as trimming. I am myself dead against any unfair means by which an expert exhibitor can defeat the novice, but there cannot be anything unsportsmanlike in showing one's favourite at its very best so long as fair means only are employed. I have often thought that the most extremely simple thing

CH. TONE JERRY.

I know is to put a dog down in good form; and my own view is that the right down bad condition in which many show Terriers are benched is due more to laziness than ignorance. At eight months old your Terrier should be stripped of his coat all over, using the thumb and finger only. After that it is only a question of using the brush and hound glove, good food, comfortable sleeping quarters, and judicious exercise. In four weeks, generally, the coat will be on again, and the pride of your kennel, if he is good enough, fit to battle with the best. Genius has often been baldly quoted as the art of taking pains. A fancier need not be a genius to breed a great dog; but it is imperative that he should spare no pains in bringing him to the acme of show form and condition. And let me say here that those who preach the cult of perfect show form are the best friends of the novice exhibitor. Canine history abounds with instances of novice exhibitors showing really great dogs in right down bad form, with the result that a perfectly trained dog, in the pink of condition, but inferior on aggregate show points, has pegged the other back, and the novice with an imperfect knowledge of the *rara avis* which he has harboured unawares, listens to the voice of the knowing dealer, and parts with his Terrier, to his afterwards eternal regret. All this could easily have been avoided had he had the nous to have benched the dog in good form. In these days of specialist clubs and their multiplication there is no excuse for the novice not learning all there is to be learnt, more particularly of the breed under notice, branches of the parent club having been formed for entirely educational purposes.

CHAPTER VI.

Some Important Back Blood of the Breed.

I suppose that Ch. Tommy Tucker was about the best all round sporting Terrier ever bred; he had very few chances at stud, more's the pity. Ch. Otley Chevin was another gamey Terrier who quickly set all dogs by the ears as soon as he stepped into the ring. I never saw Airedale Jerry, but Mr. John Horrocks tells me that he was weak in face and big enough in ears, but a grand bodied and coloured dog, so no doubt his great son, Ch. Cholmondeley Briar, got his wonderful tan and body from old Jerry. Luce, the dam of the above-mentioned champion, was a particularly small-eared bitch, with great jaw power and indifferent legs and feet.

I have had many different versions given me of the qualities of Ch. Newbold Test. The weight of evidence is in favour of Test being on hound-like lines, with rather large ears and light eyes. Ch. Rover was a grandly-built Terrier, but with an awful coat.

Briar Test was a magnificently-proportioned Terrier, with that real barrel jaw that we hear about so often but seldom see; his ears were very small and well carried, splendidly boned, and dead straight. I don't know why he did not finish a champion, he was surely good enough; in fact, coat, which was sheep-like, was his only '' out.''

So very few people have ever seen Betty, the dam of Ch. Master Briar, that perhaps a short notice of her would be welcome. Faults: On the small side, bar that I have never seen a sweeter or truer-made bitch; very small well-carried ears right on top of her grand coat,

BRIAR TEST.

and colour; a Terrier head with the real hard expression about; small, dark eyes, full of fire and intelligence, and a perfectly-shaped body. Small wonder that in alliance with Briar Test she should have produced Master Briar; a great many of her excellences she got from her dam, Venom. Mr. J. H. Rockett, who has the great credit of producing Master Briar, bred another puppy in Betty's next litter quite as good as that celebrity, thus proving that Briar was no fluke.

Briar Test's litter brother, Stamper, deserves mention. His influence is most marked in the way of head and ears. He had much the same great jaw power, but not combined with the beautiful quality of his more distinguished brother; great bone, but indifferent colour; light and wavy. Burnley Crack was a very neat Terrier-like dog, with a perfect eye, which he has handed down with unfailing regularity to his numerous sons and daughters. Ch. Rustic Twig, a big fellow, on powerful lines, rare legs and feet, and sound colour. Ch. Rustic Kitty was on the other hand, very small, and low to ground, very good coat, colour, ears, and fair head. She would best be described as being just a fair bitch all over. Clonmel Queen, who is in three parts of the pedigrees of to-day, was a grand bodied animal, head only fair, rather short from eye to nose, ears largeish, a short backed one but not at all a show specimen.

Rock Ferry Test, who was a great deal used at stud at one time, was something of a sensation in his day. Bought by Sam Wilson, at a low figure, he was sold to Mr. Thos. Baines, who at that time was making a start in this breed, and a very bad start it proved, as "Test" was unable to get into the money at Llangollen on his first appearance for his new owner. Rock Ferry Test, truth to say, was something of a flatcatcher, a fetching front, long head, but nothing in it; an awful coat, quite sheep-like, on a long back. He proved his blood, how-

ever, by siring Ch. Rock Salt; but my own idea was that
Marsden Luce, his dam, was in a great measure
responsible for that good dog's many excellences.
Marsden Luce was on the small side, but all a Terrier,
with a hard black coat, black eye, beautiful ears, and a
rare shape. Mention of this bitch recalls the name of
Ch. Rock Princess, one of the best bitches of the past
decade. She possessed all her sire's, Accrington Rough,
high quality; rare neck, shoulders, legs and feet, and
one of the best expressions I have ever seen. She had
a tragic ending—she was sold to Mr. Foxhall Keene, but
something happened to her on board the liner, and she
never survived the journey.

Chippenham Daisy is a matron who has a great deal of
her classic blood about. Absolutely perfect in body,
shape, coat, colour, head, ears, and legs and feet, but
the almost perfect picture was marred by a light, staring
eye.

Dumbarton Conqueror is in the pedigree of not a few:
best front possible; grand shoulders, but too dark in tan,
and quite a foreign expression.

Rock Ferry Sensation was a lovely moulded Terrier;
her head, however, was rather off in shape, and her eyes
not pleasing in colour or expression.

STUDHOLME SVENGALI.

CHAPTER VII.

Some American Fanciers and Their Dogs.

English fanciers are none too well catered for in the way of a supply of news concerning their breed from the United States and Canada. Most fanciers are familiar with the name of Mr. Clement B. Newbold, the owner of Ch. Clonmel Monarch, Broadlands Bilbery, Briar Vampire, and some brood bitches who, in alliance with Monarch or his numerous sons, keep throwing good stock. Mr. Newbold does not exhibit much nowadays, but Mr. Eugene Newbold has a nomination which can mostly take a cut at the winner, if not absolutely scoring. Another Philadelphia fancier who has rapidly forced his way to the front rank—Mr. Russell H. Johnston— possesses a really powerful kennel, which can hold its end up in the strongest competition. His friend and partner, Mr. William Barclay, has had the most striking success in his breeding efforts. He seems to have based his groundwork upon Monarch, and he has a great little dog in Wynhill Hill Tackle, who is very prolific in getting winners, and is inbred to Monarch. Daniel Buckley is certainly one of the oldest fanciers in the United States, and but for ill-health would have had a large say in the prize list. Bronside Monarch was certainly more than plausible.

The Hastings kennels were a power to be reckoned with, but of late have slackened, and have not had near such a good season as formerly. Mr. Arthur Merritt is a Yorkshireman bred and born, and has carried with him to the land of his adoption the love for the Yorkshire

a

breed of Terrier which time is unable to quench. Ch.
The New King, his son Prince Hal, Dumbarton Ranger,
and Clonmel Majesty are only a few of the good ones
owned by this Anglo-American fancier.

Mr. Philip French is another Boston fancier who
keeps pegging away, and if he would only put his
Amazement to Clonmel Monarch, would surely breed a
"Marvel." Mr. W. H. Whitten, another fancier who
has already made his mark by breeding that charming
bitch, Ingalflora, who has beaten most of her sex in that
country.

Jos. A. Laurin, of Montreal, certainly takes the palm
as a buyer of Airedales. Hundreds of brood bitches, and
the Champions Dumbarton Lass, Willow Nut, and Lucky
Baldwin are names to conjure with in both Continents.

Mr. Theo. Offerman's first purchase was, we believe,
Clonmel Floriform, and this dog must have been the best
doggy investment Mr. Offerman ever made. He had a
great time, and finished up by beating all the champions
at New York in February, 1904. He has also been a
stud success. Ch. Dumbarton Sceptre and Ch. Tone
Masterpiece were the next two of Mr. Offerman's
choosing, and rare and well have they repaid his pluck
in their purchase. Mr. Bunnell and Mr. Boorum, a
brace of very enthusiastic New York fanciers, are
breeders who have had the wisdom to get the right
stuff to breed from, and this combination is likely to
go far in the production of high-class stock in the future.
Mr. J. H. Brookfield, the able Secretary of the Airedale
Club, has been for some years pegging away, and is evidently a stayer, and it is a proverb that the victory is
not always with the slap-dash brigade. Mr. Brookfield
will get right there some day. Mr. C. O'Donnel did a
fair share of winning in 1903 with some of Mr. John-
stone's reds.

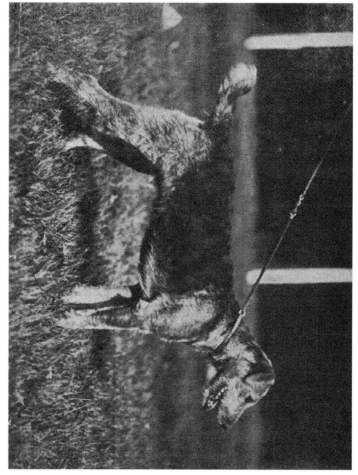

KISMET FLASHLIGHT.

Mr. John Watson was also successful with Dumbarton Ranger and Lord Raglan. Mr. John Lorillard, Arden, who was virtually the pioneer of the breed, seldom or never shows, but his services are in great request as an adjudicator. Lynford Biddle representatives are frequently in the money. Mr. Foxhall Keene seems to have virtually retired from the fray, and De Witt Cochrane judges more than he shows. Mr. Frank Dole has shown a fair one in Edgewood Conqueror. Does this portend a change of fancies ? Mr. John Gough is mostly at the money end of the prize list. I have heard that Black Queen is a good one. Dr. H. Jarrett is one of the oldest fanciers, and his determination to own some of the best remains undiminished.

The following is the best description (an American one) of the Airedale that I have ever read : —

THE AIREDALE TERRIER.

" Fidelis, Audax et Paratus."

This is the largest and hardiest breed of Terrier yet produced, and owes his popularity to his adaptability to every kind of sport. He is a natural hunter, has a keen nose, and is easily broken to gun. He will do all the work of a Spaniel, and can be taught to drive cattle like a Collie. A capital water dog and retriever, he is a first-rate workman on shore, and when hunting along the banks of a river there are few dogs that can equal him, for his close, wiry jacket enables him to withstand the effects of the wet, whilst being such a big dog he is more than a match for any sort of vermin he may fall across. Rats they will destroy as quick as one can wink, being almost as rapid in their movements as a mongoose. They will hunt rabbits with the zeal of a Foxhound or Beagle, tree a coon, and kill him when he drops ; and to muskrats, water rats, and weasels they are sure death. No hole is too deep in the water for them to follow their quarry, for hours they will work indefatigably, and woe betide the object of their search when found. In England, in addition to being used on vermin, they are taught to retrieve ducks, geese, and swans, and on account of their size and strength, no sea is too rough for them when in pursuit of wounded wild fowl. They are also easily broken to the gun for covert shooting, and when a badger is to be " induced " to come out of his box, the Airedale either brings him out or is a dead dog. In point of disposition, no dog could be possessed of more qualities that endear him to his owner; he is far from quarrelsome with other dogs, is inclined to shun them at walk; yet let another dog dispute his right to advance, he is up and at it in a moment. Then his opponent must look to himself, however big or strong he may be. The Airedale's jaw, of wonderful length and punishing power, soon does its work, and he will die ere he turns tail. At home he is docile in the extreme, fond of children, and a good guardian, and obedient to a wonderful degree, which, coupled with an intelligence almost human, make him a most enjoyable companion. The Airedale, more-over, possesses another great recommendation in the eyes of many dog lovers, this being the possession of a very hardy constitution, which causes little trouble to his breeders during the earlier stages of his career, and when grown, they can stand an unlimited amount of rough wear and tear work. He stands any climate, and is now established in the United States, Canada, South Africa, Australia, India, and on the Continent of Europe. Altogether, he is one of the most useful dogs living, and has a personality all his own.

CHAPTER VIII.

General Remarks.

The high-water mark of the breed was probably reached at the first great championship club show at the Regent's Park, London, in June, 1905—the first club show on big lines that has ever been held for the breed. The venue was charming, and the collection of specimens of the breed unquestionably the finest ever held; a record entry, in fact, for the world. The Committee of the South of England Airedale Terrier Association, with that innate love of true sport that has always distinguished them, resolved upon the selection of a Northern judge, and that doyen of the breed, Mr. Maude Barrett, of Otley, was the gentleman upon whom the choice fell. The result was, as might have been anticipated, as near faultless as judging can possibly be. Mr. Barrett is a consummate master of the cult, so error was therefore impossible or nearly so. The show is to be an annual one, so that the Airedale takes his place with the most fashionable breeds of the Terrier fancy; and if breeders will only stick to his sporting character, as well as developing mere show points, his place will in the whirligig of time inevitably be the first place. It may be thought by those who are over hasty in judgment that dogs which the writer has had the honour to own, or in partnership with Mr. E. Royston Mills, have been too freely mentioned in the historical part of this book, but it is a perfectly just and an obvious reflection that the history of the breed for the last dozen years at least has had a great deal to do with our own kennel, and, like "the King's head" in poor Uncle Dick's life, it must keep popping up when writing extensively of the Airedale Terrier.

Lightning Source UK Ltd.
Milton Keynes UK
UKHW040615070119
335119UK00001B/54/P